superb

ISBN 1 74022 428 0

Published by R&R Publications Marketing Pty. Ltd.

ABN 78 348 105 138

PO Box 254, Carlton North, Victoria 3054 Australia

Australia wide tollfree 1800 063 296

E-mail: info@randrpublications.com.au

Web: www.randrpublications.com.au

Publisher: Richard Carroll

Production Manager: Anthony Carroll

Cover Designer: Aisling Gallagher

Layout Designer: Elain Wei Voon Loh

Recipes: Concept New Zealand & R&R Kitchens

Photography: Concept New Zealand & R&R Kitchens

Proof reading: Lyn Roach

Printed through Bookbuilders, Hong Kong

Introduction

All over the world, a bowl of soup speaks of love, warmth and comfort. Just a few spoonfulls fills us with a tangible serenity, as real as the fragrant liquid that nourishes our bodies and satisfies our soul.

Soup is one of man's most basic foods. Its history streatches far into the past when soup was simply water simmered with whatever basic ingredients were available for flavour. Soup then was never about quality ingredients and complex flavours. Rather, it was simply about survival. Yet soup was still a meal shared between family members and aquaintances.

Thick hearty soups are served in the cold months to nourish and satisfy hungry children and to give energy to busy people at the end of a hectic day.

Cold refreshing soups are served in hot and humid climates to invigorate and enliven after an exhausting hot day.

Throughout the Western world soups are served as a teaser to the coming meal, while in China soup is served after the meal as an invigorating finale. In many European countries soup is served between courses to refresh the palate.

In fact soup is served more often and in many more flavour combinations throughout the world than any other meal known to man.

Techniques

While soup is very easy to make and delightfully satisfying to eat, there is no doubt that a few tricks of the trade and some handy hints will give you superior results, even if you have never made a pot of soup before.

Cookware

While quality cookware is always a joy to use, remember that soups are centuries old and most of our forefathers didn't have the pleasure of shiny new cookware and elegant cooktops. Just use whatever large saucepans or stockpots you have. If you find you need a new saucepan, purchase a high quality pot with a strong enamel or non-stick surface, or a stainless steel pot that has an insulated base. Cast iron works well too.

Ingredients

We all want to use the best, freshest ingredients when we prepare foods for our family or friends, and there is no doubt that quality ingredients contribute towards a more delicious and healthy end result. Meat, fish, poultry, spices and herbs should always be in peak condition for the best soups. Vegetables, however, can be a little wilted or past their prime. When you are about to make a soup or stock, clean out your vegetable crisper and see what has been left behind. Of course, common sense should prevail, so don't use any vegetables that smell unpleasant or are obviously mouldy.

Stocks

The basis of a quality soup is a quality stock, it's as simple as that! In years past, a good soup always began with hours of simmering simple vegetables and, perhaps, some meat bones to create a rich broth.

These days, however, if you prefer to bypass this step, there are several prepared stocks available from your local supermarket. They can be found in liquid form, as a paste or as a powder.

Generally speaking, it is much better to purchase liquid stocks as they have a true flavour and are literally ready to use. Pastes are a good option too because they are concentrated, which allows you to add as much water as necessary to dilute the flavour according to your tastes.

In our opinion, most stock powders should be avoided if the liquid or paste stocks are available. These powders are often heavily salted and therefore offer a salty rather than 'true to taste' flavour. The ratio of powder to water can be difficult to master and some brands contain artificial flavours and colours.

By far the most rewarding and delicious stock is the one you make yourself. Contrary to popular belief, stocks are not difficult to make and, although they do need to simmer for quite some time, their preparation time is minimal.

The following recipes on pages 8 and 9 will guide you through the basics of making a good stock—regardless of which type of stock you wish to make, you can follow one of these basic methods. If you have any vegetables in your refrigerator that are looking a little wilted and sad, throw these into the stockpot too as they will add extra flavour and colour.

Oh, and one other thing—remember that stocks freeze extremely well for extended periods of time, so don't be afraid to make a pot of stock when you have large amounts of vegetables, roasted meat bones or turkey frames (from the Christmas bird) on hand. Make the stock and pop it in the freezer for your future risotto or soup.

Rich Vegetable Stock

In addition to the vegetables below, you can add any other vegetables in your refrigerator that are past their prime; greens, root vegetables, corn and capsicum all work well. The stock freezes beautifully for up to 12 months.

Ingredients

2 tbsp olive oil	*1 turnip or swede*
5 cloves garlic	*3 ribs celery*
3 large carrots	*10 mushrooms*
3 large onions	*4 tomatoes*
2 leeks, well washed	*10 sprigs parsley*
2 parsnips peppercorns	*1 teaspoon*
8 brussel sprouts	*4 bay leaves*

Method

Wash all the vegetables and slice or chop roughly. Heat the olive oil in a large stockpot and sauté all the vegetables for 20 minutes until they begin to develop a golden colour on the surface. Add the parsley, peppercorns, bay leaves and water to cover (about 4 litres) and bring to the boil. Simmer for 3 hours, skimming the surface to remove any scum that accumulates. Add salt to taste, then simmer for a further

few minutes if you would like a more intense flavour. Allow to cool then strain, pressing on the solids. Use within 3 days or freeze for up to 12 months.

Chicken, Beef and Fish Stocks

Common Ingredients

2 carrots
3 onions
1 leek
4 ribs celery
8 sprigs parsley
1 tsp peppercorns

Chicken Stock

To the above ingredients, add 2kg of chicken frames or wings and place all the vegetables and chicken in a large stockpot. Add water to generously cover the ingredients (about 4 litres). Bring to the boil then simmer for 2–3 hours, skimming the scum off the surface as it rises to the top. Add salt to taste, then strain the stock through a sieve lined with paper towels or cheesecloth. Place in a large saucepan and chill until the fat solidifies on the surface. Remove the fat and use the stock or freeze.

Beef Stock

Place 2kg of beef bones in a roasting pan and roast at 220°C for one hour. Then place in a large stockpot with the common vegetable ingredients. Cover with cold water (about 4 litres), bring to the boil and simmer for 2–3 hours, skimming the scum off the surface as it rises to the top. Add salt to taste, then strain through a sieve lined with paper towels or cheesecloth. Place in a large saucepan and chill until the fat solidifies on the surface. Remove the fat and use the stock or freeze.

Fish Stock

Using the common vegetable ingredients, follow the recipe for Rich Vegetable Stock then, when adding the vegetables to the stockpot, also add 2kg of flathead heads (or other white ocean fish heads). Cover with cold water (about 3 litres), bring to the boil and simmer for 2 hours, skimming the scum off the surface as it rises to the top. Strain through a sieve lined with paper towels or cheesecloth, place in a large saucepan and chill until the fat solidifies on the surface. Remove the fat then use the stock or freeze.

One Final Note

You will notice that the recipes in this book usually serve 4–6 or more people. This is because soup generally keeps very well and is often even better on the second or third day. Therefore, one recipe can offer you sustenance and an easy nutritional choice for several meals. If you prefer not to make such a large serve, or if you are cooking for only one or two people, all these recipes can be halved successfully.

Carrot and Orange Soup

1 tbsp vegetable oil
2 leeks, thinly sliced
6 large carrots, sliced
2 tbsp curry powder
1 tbsp finely grated lemon rind
1 cup orange juice
1 1/2 cups coconut milk
2 cups vegetable stock
freshly ground black pepper
1/3 cup natural yoghurt
100g cashew nuts, roasted and chopped
1 tbsp chopped fresh mint

serves 4

1 Heat oil in a large saucepan. Add leeks and cook over a medium heat, stirring, for 5 minutes or until golden.

2 Add carrots, curry powder, lemon rind and orange juice to pan, bring to the boil and simmer for 10 minutes or until carrots are soft.

3 Stir in coconut milk and stock and simmer for 10 minutes longer.

4 Remove pan from heat and set aside to cool slightly. Place soup mixture, in batches, in a food processor or blender and process until smooth.

5 Return soup to a clean saucepan and heat over a medium heat, stirring, for 4–5 minutes or until hot. Season to taste with black pepper. Serve soup topped with yoghurt, cashew nuts and mint.

Garlic and Parsley Soup

1 bead garlic, cloves separated and unpeeled
6 cups vegetable stock
1/4 tsp dried sage
1/4 tsp dried thyme
1 small bay leaf
3 sprigs fresh parsley
2 large potatoes, diced
pinch saffron powder
1 bunch fresh parsley, finely chopped
freshly ground black pepper

serves 6

1 Bring a saucepan of water to the boil, add garlic cloves and boil for 30 seconds. Drain, rinse under cold running water and peel.

2 Place garlic, stock, sage, thyme, bay leaf and parsley sprigs in a large saucepan and bring to the boil. Reduce heat and simmer for 30 minutes.

3 Add potatoes and saffron to stock mixture and simmer for 15–20 minutes or until potatoes are tender. Remove bay leaf and discard. Remove pan from heat and set aside to cool slightly.

4 Place soup in batches in a food processor or blender and process until smooth. Return soup to a clean saucepan, bring to the boil and simmer for 2–3 minutes or until soup is hot. Stir in chopped parsley and season to taste with black pepper.

Vegetable Soup with Pistou

1 tbsp olive oil & 2 onions, chopped & 2 zucchini, sliced

2 leeks, sliced & 1/2 tsp dried thyme

1 tsp chopped fresh thyme or 3 stalks celery

2 large potatoes & 2 carrots, diced

250g green beans, cut into 2 1/2 cm pieces

440g canned lima, butter, red kidney or mixed beans, drained

8 cups water

freshly ground black pepper

Pistou

1 bunch basil, leaves removed and stems discarded

2 cloves garlic, chopped

125g Parmesan cheese, chopped

1/4 cup olive oil

1 Heat 1 tablespoon olive oil in a large saucepan over a medium heat, add onions, leeks and thyme and cook, stirring, for 5 minutes or until onions and leeks are soft.

2 Add celery, potatoes and carrots and cook, stirring, for 5 minutes. Add zucchini, green beans, canned beans and water and bring to the boil. Reduce heat and simmer for 30 minutes or until vegetables are tender. Season to taste with black pepper.

3 To make Pistou, place basil, garlic, Parmesan cheese, olive oil and black pepper to taste in a food processor or blender and process to make a paste. Just prior to serving, stir Pistou into soup.

serves 6

Quick Mushroom Soup

200g button mushrooms
2 cloves garlic
1 tbsp butter
1 packet mushroom soup mix
1 cup water
1 cup low fat milk
2 tbsp chopped parsley
freshly ground black pepper

serves 2–3

1 Wipe mushrooms and slice thinly. Crush, peel and finely chop garlic.

2 Melt butter in a medium saucepan. Sauté mushrooms and garlic in butter for 2–3 minutes.

3 Mix soup mix and water together. Pour into the saucepan and bring to the boil. Add milk. Bring to the boil. Reduce heat and simmer for 3–4 minutes.

4 Serve garnished with chopped parsley and freshly ground black pepper.

Fish with Tomato and Dill

3 medium tomatoes

750g freshwater fish fillets

6 cups chicken stock

2 tbsp chopped fresh dill

salt and pepper

extra fresh dill

serves 6

1 Chop tomatoes into wedges. Cut fish into large bite-sized chunks. Boil stock. Add fish, and turn down to simmer for 6 minutes. Skim surface froth and add tomatoes, dried dill and salt and pepper to taste.

2 Simmer a little longer until fish is cooked but not breaking up. Serve in large bowl or individual bowls and garnish with fresh dill.

This is a chunky soup is a good starter or part of a multi-coursed Vietnamese meal. It also makes a family lunch or dinner served with fresh baguettes and a salad.

Beef Pho

225g thick steak in one piece

rice noodles

455g flat, thick, dried noodles

2 tbsp fish sauce

$^1/_2$ cup of bean sprouts

1 brown onion, thinly sliced

3 spring onions, finely chopped

$^1/_2$ cup fresh coriander, torn into sprigs

$^1/_2$ cup Vietnamese mint leaves, chopped

1 small red chilli, seeded and sliced into rings

2 limes cut into wedges

1 To make stock, pour water into a large pot and add shin bones and gravy beef, bring to the boil. Skim off foaming scum from surface. Turn heat to medium-low, partly cover and simmer for 2 hours, skimming often. Add remaining stock ingredients. Simmer another 90 minutes and remove from heat.

2 Drain through a fine sieve, reserving stock. Discard bones, carrots, onion and spices. When cool, skim fat from stock. Cut gravy beef finely across the grain. Slice steak to paper thin slices and set aside.

3 Soak rice noodles in warm water for about 20 minutes until soft. Drain and set aside.

4 Return stock pot to boil with fish sauce then reduce heat to very low. Fill a separate large pot three-quarters full of water and bring to the boil.

5 Add dried noodles and washed bean sprouts. Continue boiling until noodles are tender but not mushy. Bean sprouts should retain some crispness.

6 Pour boiling stock into 6 serving bowls, add drained noodles then top equally with shin meat, raw onion rings, chopped spring onions, and raw steak slices, and garnish with coriander and mint leaves.

Diners may help themselves to chilli rings and lime wedges. This recipe is also good with to chicken which takes less time to cook.

serves 6

Stock:

12 cups water

1kg shin beef bones

340g gravy beef

1 large brown, unpeeled onion, halved

3 medium pieces unpeeled ginger, sliced pinch of salt

1 cinnamon stick

6 whole cloves

6 peppercorns

6 coriander seeds

4 whole star anise

2 unpeeled carrots, cut into chunks

Asparagus and Crab Meat Soup (Mang Tay Nau Cua)

4 cups chicken broth

1 tbsp plus 2 tsp fish sauce

1/2 tsp sugar & 1/4 tsp salt

1 tbsp vegetable oil

6 shallots, chopped

2 cloves garlic, chopped

225g crab meat

freshly ground black pepper

2 tbsp corn flour or arrowroot, mixed with 2 tbsp cold water

1 egg, lightly beaten

425g white asparagus spears, cut into 2 1/2 cm sections, reserves canning liquid

1 tbsp shredded coriander

1 spring onion, thinly sliced

serves 4–6

1 Combine broth, 1 tablespoon of fish sauce, sugar and salt in a 3 1/2 litre soup pot. Bring to the boil. Reduce the heat and simmer.

2 Meanwhile, heat oil in a skillet. Add shallots and garlic and stir-fry until aromatic. Add crab meat, the remaining 2 teaspoons of fish sauce and black pepper to taste. Stir-fry over high heat for 1 minute. Set aside.

3 Bring the soup to a boil. Add corn flour mixture and stir gently until the soup thickens and is clear. While the soup is actively boiling, add egg and stir gently.

4 Continue to stir for about 1 minute. Add crab meat mixture and asparagus with its canning liquid. Cook gently until heated through.

5 Transfer the soup to a heated tureen. Sprinkle on the coriander, spring onion and freshly ground black pepper.

If white asparagus is unavailable, use frozen or fresh asparagus to the broth from the very beginning and cook until tender, before adding the remaining ingredients.

Hot and Sour Fish Soup

1 Remove head, fins and tail from fish and cut into 8–10 large pieces. Combine fish, fish sauce, pepper and spring onion, allow to marinate for 15 minutes.

2 Place water in a large saucepan and bring to the boil. Add the fish with its juices and lemongrass. Reduce heat and simmer for 20 minutes.

3 Meanwhile, combine tamarind pulp and boiling water and allow to soak for 15 minutes. Strain mixture through a fine sieve and discard pulp.

4 Add the tamarind liquid, sugar, bamboo shoots, pineapple and tomatoes to the pan. Simmer for 4–5 minutes until fish is tender.

5 Divide bean sprouts amongst serving bowls and spoon hot soup over. Sprinkle with fresh herbs and deep-fried shallots. Serve with lime wedges and sliced chilli on the side.

serves 4–6

1kg firm-fleshed fish such as red snapper

1 1/2 tbsp nuoc cham

1/4 tsp white pepper

1 spring onion, chopped

6 cups water

2 stalks lemongrass, cut into 5cm lengths and crushed lightly

55g tamarind pulp

3/4 cup boiling water & 1 tbsp sugar

3/4 cup sliced bamboo shoots

1 cup sliced pineapple & 1 cup beans prouts

2 tomatoes, cut into wedges

mixed Vietnamese herbs such as coriander, bitter herb, Asian basil

deep fried 2 shallots

lime wedges & sliced chilli

Cabbage Parcels in Soup

24 cabbage leaves

6 spring onions

4 tbsp coriander, finely chopped

1 cup pork, minced

1/2 cup prawns, minced

6 1/4 cups chicken or pork stock

2 1/2 tbsp fish sauce

serves 6

1 Blanch cabbage leaves in boiling water and cut away any tough sections from their bases.

2 Cut white ends from spring onions and finely chop 4 white heads. Slice 2 for garnish. Halve, lengthwise green stalks, into strips.

3 Mix well chopped spring onions and 2 tablespooons of coriander with pork and prawns. Season with pepper.

4 Into each cabbage leaf, place 1 tablespoon of mixture. Fold the leaf base over then the outer edges and roll up. Carefully tie up each roll with a length of green spring onion and place parcels gently into boiling stock to cook for 6 minutes.

5 Lift parcels into bowls, pour a cup of stock over each and garnish with remaining sliced spring onions and coriander. Dip rolls into fish sauce when eating.

Duck and Nut Soup & Mushroom and Barley Soup

Duck and Nut Soup

1 Cut duck into bite-sized pieces. Fry in a little peanut oil until golden. Boil stock or water with salt. Add duck and simmer for 45 minutes. Skim till broth is clear.

2 Add nuts and simmer another 45 minutes. Add lychees or loganberries 5 minutes before serving. Garnish with coriander leaves.

serves 6

6 pieces duck or chicken
peanut oil & 2 tsp salt
8 cups water or stock
2 cups mixed nuts, crushed
1/2 can of lychees or loganberries, drained
fresh coriander for garnish

Mushroom and Barley Soup

1 Place mushrooms, tomato, carrots, onion, celery, parsley, barley and water in a large saucepan and bring to the boil. Reduce heat, cover and simmer for 1 hour or until barley is tender. Season to taste with black pepper.

serves 4

500g button mushrooms, sliced
1 tomato & 2 carrots, chopped
1 onion, chopped
2 stalks celery, chopped
2 tbsp chopped fresh parsley
1/2 cup barley
6 cups water
freshly ground black pepper

Vermicelli and Chicken Soup

1 cup chicken breast chunks

225g Chinese mung bean vermicelli

1/2 cup of dried wood ear mushrooms, soaked or 1/2 cup canned button mushrooms, sliced

salt to taste

1/2 tsp black or white pepper

2 tbsp spring onions, chopped

Stock:

8 cups water & 3 tsp fish sauce

1 onion, quartered

1 1/2 kg pork bones

455g chicken wings, bones and/or leftover meat scraps

455g of 2 of the following: whole carrot, quartered cauliflower, whole green beans and/or quarter of a cabbage

1 Use packaged stock or make stock by boiling all ingredients together then simmering for 1 hour. Strain reduced stock and discard the bones and vegetables.

2 Boil chicken chunks in stock for 15 minutes, skimming scum from the surface. Add vermicelli and softened dried, mushrooms, removed stalks or canned mushrooms and cook until vermicelli is done.

3 Serve, season with salt and pepper and sprinkle with chopped spring onion.

serves 6

Hot and Sour Seafood Soup

1 Place shallots, chillies, lime leaves, ginger and stock in a saucepan and bring to the boil over a high heat. Reduce heat and simmer for 3 minutes.

2 Add fish, prawns, mussels and mushrooms and cook for 3–5 minutes or until fish and seafood are cooked, discard any mussels that do not open after 5 minutes cooking. Stir in lime juice and fish sauce. To serve, ladle soup into bowls, scatter with coriander leaves and accompany with lime wedges.

Straw mushrooms are one of the most popular mushrooms used in Asian cooking and in the West are readily available canned. Oyster mushrooms are also known as abalone mushrooms and range in colour from white to grey to pale pink. Their shape is similar to that of an oyster shell and they have a delicate flavour. Oyster mushrooms should not be eaten raw as some people are allergic to them in the uncooked state.

4 red or golden shallots, sliced
2 fresh green chillies, chopped
6 kaffir lime leaves
4 slices fresh ginger
8 cups fish, chicken or vegetable stock
250g boneless firm fish fillets, cut into chunks
12 medium uncooked prawns, shelled and deveined
12 mussels, scrubbed and beards removed
125g oyster or straw mushrooms
3 tablespoons lime juice
2 tbsp Thai fish sauce (nam pla)
fresh coriander leaves
lime wedges

serves 6

Chicken and Coconut Soup

3 cups coconut milk

2 cups oz water

500g chicken breast fillets, cut into 1cm thick strips

4cm piece fresh galangal or ginger, sliced, or 6 slices bottled galangal

2 stalks fresh lemon grass, cut into 4cm pieces, or 1 tsp dried lemon grass, soaked in hot water until soft

1 fresh coriander root, bruised

4 kaffir lime leaves, shredded

3 fresh red chillies, seeded and chopped

2 tablespoons Thai fish sauce (nam pla)

2 tbsp lemon juice

fresh coriander leaves

serves 6

1 Place coconut milk and water in a saucepan and bring to the boil over a medium heat, add chicken, galangal or ginger, lemon grass, coriander root and lime leaves and simmer for 6 minutes.

2 Stir in chillies, fish sauce and lemon juice. To serve, ladle into bowls and scatter with coriander leaves.

This popular Thai soup is known as Tom Kha Gai. When dining in the traditional Thai manner soups are not served as a separate course but are eaten with the other dishes and rice.

Chilli Kumara Soup

6 cups chicken stock

3 stalks fresh lemon grass, bruised, or 1 1/2 tsp dried lemon grass, soaked in hot water until soft

3 fresh red chillies, halved

10 slices fresh or bottled galangal or fresh ginger

5–6 fresh coriander plants, roots washed, leaves removed and reserved

1 large kumara (orange sweet potato), peeled and cut into 2cm pieces

3/4 cup coconut cream

1 tbsp Thai fish sauce (nam pla)

serves 4

1 Place stock, lemon grass, chillies, galangal or ginger and coriander roots in a saucepan and bring to the boil over a medium heat. Add kumara (sweet potato) and simmer, uncovered, for 15 minutes or until kumara is soft.

2 Remove lemon grass, galangal or ginger and coriander roots and discard. Cool liquid slightly, then purée soup, in batches, in a food processor or blender. Return soup to a clean saucepan and stir in 125m of the coconut cream and the fish sauce. Cook, stirring, over a medium heat for 4 minutes or until heated. Stir in two-thirds of the reserved coriander leaves.

3 To serve, ladle soup into bowls, top with a little of the remaining coconut cream and scatter with remaining coriander leaves.

Aztec Flower Soup

2 tsp vegetable oil
1 onion, finely chopped
1 clove garlic, crushed
2 tbsp white rice
2 tsp chopped fresh marjoram
2 tsp chopped fresh thyme
8 cups chicken stock
12 zucchini flowers
440g cooked or canned chickpeas, rinsed and drained
250g chopped cooked chicken
1 avocado, sliced
2 jalapeño chillies, sliced
1 tbsp fresh coriander leaves
1/4 onion, chopped

serves 6

1 Heat oil in a saucepan over a medium heat, add onion and garlic and cook, stirring, for 3 minutes or until onion is soft. Add rice, marjoram, thyme and stock, bring to simmering and simmer for 15 minutes.

2 Remove the stamens and pistils from the zucchini flowers by pinching with your fingers. Check that there are no insects hidden in the petals and wash flowers by dipping into water briefly. Trim stalks and set aside.

3 Add chickpeas, chicken and zucchini flowers to soup and cook for 3 minutes or until flowers are tender.

4 To serve, ladle soup into bowls and top with avocado, chillies, coriander and onion.

Pinto Bean Soup

1 Place beans, onion, tomatoes, poblano chilli, garlic and water in a saucepan. Bring to the boil and boil for 10 minutes, then reduce heat and simmer for 1 hour or until beans are tender. Cool slightly, then purée beans and vegetables with cooking liquid in a food processor or blender.

2 Return purée to a clean saucepan, stir in stock, bring to simmering and simmer, stirring, for 10–15 minutes.

3 Heat 1cm oil in a frying pan until a cube of bread dropped in browns in 50 seconds and cook tortilla strips until golden and crisp. Drain on absorbent kitchen paper. Add ancho chillies to pan and cook until crisp, then drain and cut into thin strips.

4 To serve, ladle soup into warm bowls. Arrange tortilla and chilli strips, feta cheese and coriander on a serving platter and pass with soup to garnish.

185 g dried pinto beans, soaked overnight and drained

1 onion, quartered

3 tomatoes, roasted and peeled

1 poblano chilli, roasted and peeled & 4 cloves garlic

6 cups water

2–3 cups chicken or vegetable stock

vegetable oil for shallow-frying

6 day-old flour or corn tortillas, cut into strips

2 ancho chillies, seeded

155 g feta cheese, crumbled

2 tbsp fresh coriander leaves

serves 6

Chicken and Corn Chowder

1 tbsp vegetable oil

1 small onion, diced

250g boneless chicken breast fillets, shredded

3 potatoes, chopped

3 1/2 cups chicken stock

315g canned sweet corn kernels, drained and coarsely chopped

1 1/4 cups milk

1 bay leaf

freshly ground black pepper

1 tbsp lemon juice

2 tbsp chopped fresh parsley

1 tbsp snipped fresh chives

60g grated Parmesan cheese

serves 6

1 Heat oil in a saucepan over a medium heat, add onion and cook, stirring, for 4–5 minutes or until onion is soft. Add chicken and cook for 2 minutes longer or until chicken just changes colour.

2 Add potatoes and stock and bring to the boil. Reduce heat and simmer for 10 minutes or until potatoes are almost cooked. Stir sweet corn, milk, bay leaf and black pepper to taste into stock mixture and bring to the boil. Reduce heat and simmer for 3–4 minutes or until potatoes are cooked. Remove bay leaf. Stir in lemon juice, parsley, chives and black pepper to taste. Just prior to serving, sprinkle with Parmesan cheese.

To chop the sweet corn, place in a food processor or blender and process using the pulse button until the sweet corn is coarsely chopped. Creamed sweet corn can be used in place of the kernels if you wish. If using creamed sweet corn there is no need to chop it.

Vegetable Bean Soup

2 tbsp vegetable oil

3 onions, diced

3 carrots, diced

3 potatoes, diced

3 cups vegetable stock

315g canned cannellini beans, drained and rinsed

1/2 cup milk

2 tbsp chopped fresh dill

1 tbsp chopped fresh parsley

freshly ground black pepper

serves 4

1 Heat oil in a large saucepan over a medium heat, add onions and cook, stirring, for 5 minutes or until onions are lightly browned.

2 Add carrots, potatoes and stock and bring to the boil. Reduce heat, cover and simmer for 30 minutes or until vegetables are tender.

3 Stir in beans, milk, dill, parsley and black pepper to taste and cook, stirring frequently, for 3-4 minutes or until heated through.

Winter Vegetable Soup

2 tbsp vegetable oil
1 large onion, sliced
1 clove garlic, crushed
2 stalks celery, chopped
2 carrots, chopped
1 turnip, chopped
440g canned tomatoes, undrained and mashed
2 tbsp tomato paste
1 tbsp finely chopped fresh basil
1 tsp dried oregano
1 tsp sugar
6 cups vegetable stock
125g small pasta shells
315g canned red kidney beans, drained and rinsed
freshly ground black pepper

1 Heat oil in a large saucepan, add onion, garlic, celery, carrots and turnip and cook, stirring occasionally, for 4–5 minutes or until vegetables are just tender.

2 Stir in tomatoes, tomato paste, basil, oregano, sugar and stock and bring to the boil. Reduce heat and simmer for 30–45 minutes.

3 Stir in pasta and beans. Season to taste with black pepper and simmer, uncovered, for 30 minutes.

serves 6

Curried Lentil Soup

2 tbsp vegetable oil
1 onion, chopped
2 tsp curry powder
1/2 tsp ground cumin
1 tbsp tomato paste
6 cups vegetable stock
125g red or green lentils
1 small head broccoli, broken into florets
2 carrots, chopped
1 parsnip, chopped
1 stalk celery, chopped
freshly ground black pepper
1 tbsp chopped fresh parsley

serves 6

1 Heat oil in a large saucepan, add onion, curry powder and cumin and cook, stirring occasionally, for 4–5 minutes or until onion is soft. Stir in tomato paste and stock and bring to the boil. Reduce heat, add lentils, cover and simmer for 30 minutes.

2 Add broccoli, carrots, parsnip and celery and cook, covered, for 30 minutes longer or until vegetables are tender. Season to taste with black pepper. Just prior to serving, stir in parsley.

Hearty Bean Soup

185g dried haricot beans
1 tbsp oil
2 onions, chopped
2 cloves garlic, crushed
2 carrots, sliced
2 stalks celery, sliced
2 potatoes, chopped
440g canned tomatoes, undrained and mashed
6 cups water
2 tbsp chopped fresh parsley
freshly ground black pepper

serves 4

1 Place beans in a large bowl, cover with water and set aside to soak overnight.

2 Drain beans, place in a large saucepan with enough water to cover and bring to the boil. Boil for 10 minutes, reduce heat and simmer for 1 hour or until beans are soft. Drain and reserve 2 cups of cooking water. Place reserved cooking water and half the beans in a food processor or blender and process until smooth.

3 Heat oil in a large saucepan, add onions and garlic and cook, stirring, for 4–5 minutes or until onions are soft. Add carrots, celery, potatoes, tomatoes, water, beans and bean purée and bring to the boil. Reduce heat and simmer for 20 minutes or until vegetables are tender. Stir in parsley and season to taste with black pepper.

Fresh Spring Green Soup

8 dried shiitake mushrooms

8 cups light vegetable or chicken stock

6 cloves garlic, peeled

50g piece ginger, sliced

1 bunch silverbeet, washed and sliced

3 zucchini, finely sliced

1 small head of broccoli, divided into tiny florets

200g peas, shelled

4 spring onions, sliced thinly diagonally

100g sugar snap peas

2 handfuls baby spinach

salt and freshly ground pepper

serves 6

1 Soak the shiitake mushrooms in a small bowl of hot water until soft, about 20 minutes. Drain, discarding the water, and then slice the mushrooms into thin strips.

2 Place the stock in a large saucepan with the garlic and ginger and bring to the boil. Simmer for 15 minutes. Discard the garlic and ginger.

3 Add the mushrooms, sliced silverbeet, sliced zucchini, broccoli florets and shelled peas and simmer for 8–10 minutes.

4 Add the spring onions, sugar snap peas and the baby spinach and simmer for two minutes.

5 Season to taste with salt and pepper then serve hot with plenty of black pepper.

Cream of Lentil Soup

2 tsp vegetable oil
1 onion, chopped
2 leeks, chopped
2 cloves garlic, crushed
315g green lentils
6 cups vegetable stock or water
12 rocket leaves, roughly chopped
1 tbsp lemon juice
1/2 cup cream (single) or 1/2 cup natural yoghurt

serves 6

1 Heat oil in a large saucepan. Add onion, leeks and garlic and cook over a medium heat, stirring constantly, for 5 minutes or until onions are golden.

2 Stir in lentils and stock or water and bring to the boil. Reduce heat and simmer for 30 minutes or until lentils are tender. Add rocket and lemon juice and simmer for 5 minutes longer. Remove pan from heat and set aside to cool slightly.

3 Place lentil mixture, in batches, in a food processor or blender and process until smooth.

4 Return soup to a clean saucepan, bring to the boil and simmer over a medium heat for 2–3 mins or until soup is hot. Stir in cream or yoghurt.

Snow Pea Soup

1 Melt butter in a large saucepan. Add leeks and garlic and cook over a medium heat, stirring, for 4 minutes or until leeks are soft.

2 Stir in stock or water and snow peas, bring to simmering and simmer for 20 minutes. Remove pan from heat and set aside to cool slightly. Place soup mixture, in batches, in a food processor or blender and process until smooth. Push mixture through a sieve.

3 Return purée to a clean saucepan, stir in cream or milk, mint and black pepper to taste. Bring to simmering and simmer for 2 minutes or until soup is hot.

4 To make Cheese Toasts, toast bread slices under a preheated medium grill until golden on one side. Place cream cheese, Parmesan cheese, Swiss cheese and black peppercorns in a bowl and mix to combine. Spread cheese mixture over untoasted side of bread and cook under grill until cheese melts. Serve with hot soup.

15g butter

2 leeks, chopped

1 clove garlic, crushed

6 cups vegetable stock or water

375g snow peas, trimmed and halved

3/4 cup cream (single) or milk

1 tbsp chopped fresh mint

freshly ground black pepper

Cheese Toasts

1 small French stick, cut into slices

100g cream cheese

45g grated Parmesan cheese

45g grated Swiss cheese

1 teaspoon crushed black peppercorn

serves 6

Chunky Lamb Soup

30g butter

500g lamb fillet, cut into 2cm cubes

1 large onion, chopped

1 tbsp chopped fresh parsley

2 tsp paprika

1 tsp saffron powder

1 tsp ground black pepper

1.5 litres lamb or chicken stock

60g chickpeas, soaked overnight in water to cover

500g tomatoes, peeled, seeded and chopped

4 tbsp lemon juice

60g long-grain rice

serves 6

1 Melt the butter in a large saucepan over moderate heat. Add lamb cubes, onion, parsley, paprika, saffron and pepper. Cook for 5 minutes, stirring frequently. Add the stock.

2 Drain chickpeas and add them to pan with tomatoes and lemon juice. Bring to the boil, boil for 10 minutes, then cover pan and simmer mixture for 1–1 1/4 hours.

3 Stir in rice. Cook for 15–20 minutes or until tender. Serve at once, in heated bowls.

Curried Pumpkin Soup

- 1 tbsp polyunsaturated oil
- 1 large onion, chopped
- 1/2 tsp ground coriander
- 1/2 tsp ground cumin
- 1/2 tsp chilli powder
- 1 kg pumpkin, peeled and seeds removed
- 4 cups chicken stock
- freshly ground black pepper

serves 4

1 Heat oil in a large saucepan. Cook onion, coriander, cumin and chilli powder until onion softens.

2 Cut pumpkin into cubes and add to saucepan with stock. Cook pumpkin for 20 minutes or until tender, then cool slightly. Transfer soup in batches to a food processor or blender and process until smooth.

3 Return soup to a rinsed saucepan and heat. Season to taste with pepper.

Mixed Bean Soup

90g dried red kidney beans
90g dried cannellini beans
2 tbsp olive oil
60g bacon, chopped
1 onion, chopped
1 clove garlic, crushed
3 stalks celery, sliced
2 carrots, chopped
2 potatoes, chopped
6 cups chicken or vegetable stock
440g canned tomatoes, undrained and mashed
1/4 cabbage, finely shredded
60g small pasta shapes or rice
1 tsp dried mixed herbs
freshly ground black pepper
grated Parmesan cheese

1 Place red kidney and cannellini beans in a bowl. Cover with cold water and set aside to soak overnight. Drain.

2 Heat oil in a saucepan over a medium heat, add bacon, onion and garlic and cook, stirring, for 5 minutes or until onion is tender. Add celery, carrots and potatoes and cook for 1 minute longer.

3 Stir in stock, tomatoes, cabbage, pasta or rice, red kidney and cannellini beans, herbs and black pepper to taste and bring to the boil. Boil for 10 minutes, then reduce heat and simmer, stirring occasionally, for 1 hour or until beans are tender. Sprinkle with Parmesan cheese and serve.

This minestrone-style soup is delicious served with hot crusty bread. Extra vegetables of your choice may be added – it is a good way to use up odds and ends.

serves 4

Roasted Eggplant Soup

1 Place eggplant and red capsicum, skin side up under a preheated hot grill and cook for 10 minutes or until flesh is soft and skins are blackened. Peel away blackened skin and roughly chop flesh.

2 Heat oil in a large saucepan over a medium heat. Add garlic and tomatoes and cook, stirring, for 2 minutes. Add eggplant, red capsicum, stock and black pepper, bring to simmer and leave for 4 minutes. Remove pan from heat and set aside to cool slightly.

3 Place vegetables and stock in batches in food processor or blender and process until smooth. Return mixture to a clean pan, bring to simmer over a medium heat and simmer for 3–5 minutes or until heated through.

This soup can be made the day before and reheated when required.

1 kg eggplant, halved

1 red capsicum, halved

1 tsp olive oil

2 cloves garlic, crushed

4 tomatoes, peeled and chopped

3 cups vegetable stock

2 tsp crushed black peppercorns

serves 6

Minestrone

2 tbsp butter & 2 cloves garlic, crushed

2 small onions, finely chopped & 4 rashers bacon, chopped

250g bacon bones, 150g red kidney beans & 100g haricot beans, soaked overnight

1/2 small cabbage, roughly chopped & 100g spinach, washed and chopped

3 medium-sized potatoes, peeled and chopped

2 medium-sized carrots, peeled and diced

150g fresh or frozen peas, shelled & 1 stalk celery, chopped

2 tbsp parsley, finely chopped

2 litres chicken stock

salt to taste

100g tomato and cheese tortellini

50g pasta of your choice

fresh Parmesan cheese

1 Heat butter and add garlic, onion, bacon and bones. Sauté 4–5 minutes.

2 Add all other ingredients except pasta and bring to the boil. Allow to simmer covered for approximately 90 minutes.

3 Remove and discard bacon bones.

4 Stir in both pastas and cook until al dente.

To serve, sprinkle with a generous helping of Parmesan and a good crusty loaf of your favourite bread.

serves 4

Chicken Minestrone

- olive oil spray
- 1 onion, finely chopped
- 1 clove garlic, chopped
- 1 stick celery, diced
- 1 carrot, peeled and diced
- 400g can peeled tomatoes (no added salt)
- 4 cups water
- freshly ground black pepper
- 1 tsp dried oregano
- 1 tsp mixed spice
- 2 tbsp chopped parsley
- 85g cut macaroni
- ¼ cabbage, shredded
- 145g frozen baby peas
- 200g chicken stirfry or chicken breast, chopped

serves 4–6

1 Lightly spray base of large saucepan with olive oil spray. Add onion and garlic, stirring over heat until they colour a little. Add celery and carrot and continue to stir over heat for 1 minute.

2 Chop tomatoes and add to the saucepan with the juice. Stir in water, pepper, oregano, spice and parsley. Bring to the boil and add the macaroni, stir until soup returns to the boil, turn down to a simmer and cook for 15 minutes.

3 Stir in cabbage, peas and chicken stirfry. Simmer for 15–20 minutes. Serve hot with crusty bread.

Left-over soup may be frozen for later use.

Spanish Fish Soup with Saffron

2 tbsp olive oil
2 large carrots, finely chopped
3 leeks, finely sliced and well washed
1 red capsicum, chopped
1 green capsicum, chopped
1 tbsp Spanish paprika
large pinch of saffron threads
2 cups white wine
3 cups fish stock
400g firm white fish fillets
400g prawns, shelled and deveined
400g baby calamari or squid
2 tbsp chopped parsley
1 lemon, cut into wedges

serves 4

1 Heat olive oil in a large saucepan and add carrots, leeks and capsicum and sauté until softened (about 10 minutes). Add paprika and saffron, and continue to cook for a few minutes more.

2 Add wine and stock and bring to the boil, simmering for 15 minutes.

3 Add diced fish, shelled prawns and squid and simmer for a further 5 minutes.

4 Garnish with some chopped parsley and a squeeze of lemon.

Almond Soup

200g almonds

1 clove garlic, peeled

1 tbsp finely chopped parsley

8 slices stale bread, preferably brown bread

1/3 cup olive oil

1 tsp ground cumin

1/2 tsp saffron

4 cups good chicken stock

1 cup milk

salt and pepper

serves 4

1 Fry almonds, garlic, parsley and 4 slices of bread in about 4 tbsp of oil. When golden, put the contents of the pan in a food processor and liquidise with cumin, saffron and a little stock. Put in a saucepan, pour in remaining stock and milk, season with salt and pepper and bring to the boil. Lower the heat and cook slowly for about 15 minutes.

2 Meanwhile, fry remaining bread slices in remaining olive oil until crisp and golden.

3 Bring the soup to the boil again and add 4 slices of fried bread. Cover, remove from the stove and leave for 5 minutes before serving.

Gazpacho

2 slices of stale bread (optional)

2kg tomatoes, washed and roughly chopped

1 cucumber, peeled and chopped

1 green capsicum, seeded and chopped

1 small onion, peeled and chopped

2 cloves garlic, peeled and chopped

5 tbsp olive oil

1–2 tbsp good wine vinegar, to taste

1 tsp cumin seeds or cumin powder

serves 6–8

1 Soak bread (if using) in a little water, and squeeze it out before using. (The bread helps to thicken the soup and give it a nice consistency).

2 Blend all vegetables and garlic in a mixer, and push through a sieve into a bowl. Use the mixer again to beat bread, oil and vinegar together. Add some of the tomatoes, the cumin seeds and salt to taste. Add a little water and mix into the bowl with the soup. Add a few ice cubes and leave to become cold. You can add more water if necessary.

Traditionally this soup was made by crushing the ingredients with a mortar and pestle and then adding cold water. Gazpacho should be served in wooden bowls and eaten with a wooden spoon. Make large quantities of gazpacho as it keeps well - but it won't last long, as you are bound to keep sipping it!

Iced Tomato Soup

1 Place all ingredients, except water, into a large bowl and allow to stand for 30 minutes to soften bread and blend flavours.

2 Purée one third of the mixture at a time in an electric blender or food processor. Pour back into a bowl and thin down to desired consistency with iced water.

3 Cover and chill well. Adjust seasoning to taste. Serve in chilled bowls or in a large bowl over ice.

4 Place garnish ingredients in separate bowls and allow each diner to add to garnish their own soup.

serves 8

3 slices bread, crusts removed

1kg tomatoes, skinned, seeded and chopped, or 2 x 400g cans of peeled tomato pieces, chopped

1 cucumber, peeled, seeded and chopped

1/2 cup chopped onions

2 cloves garlic, crushed

1/2 green capsicum, seeded and chopped

1 tsp salt, 1 tsp ground cumin & 2 tbsp olive oil

2 tbsp wine vinegar & 2–3 cups iced water

To Garnish:

1 red or green capsicum, diced

1 small cucumber, diced

1 onion, finely chopped

2 hard-boiled eggs, chopped

croutons

Spanish Pea Soup

2 cups dried green split peas
3 cups water
1 tbsp olive oil
1 tbsp Spanish paprika
2 onions, chopped
1 clove garlic, minced
1 green capsicum, chopped
1 medium carrot, thinly sliced
3 medium red potatoes, peeled and diced
8 cups chicken or vegetable stock
salt and pepper to taste
2 ears fresh corn
½ bunch chives
low fat yoghurt to garnish (optional)

serves 4

1 Pick over peas and rinse thoroughly. Place them in a large pot, cover with water and bring to the boil. Simmer for 2 minutes then remove from the heat, cover and let stand for 1 hour.

2 Meanwhile, heat oil in a large saucepan and add paprika, chopped onion and garlic and sauté for 5 minutes until the mixture is fragrant and onions have softened. Add green capsicum, carrot and cubed potato. Toss the vegetables thoroughly with the onion and paprika mixture until well coated, then continue to cook for 10 minutes, stirring continually.

3 Add stock, peas and salt and pepper to taste then simmer, uncovered, for 2–3 hours or until peas are very tender.

4 Cut kernels off corn cobs. Reserve ½ cup of corn and add the remainder to the soup and simmer for 2 minutes. Purée the soup until thick and smooth then serve with a few scattered corn kernels and some chopped chives. Garnish each plate with a teaspoon of low fat yoghurt if desired.

French Onion Soup

6 large onions

3 cloves garlic

2 tbsp oil

5 cups hot water

4 bbef stock cubes

6 x 1cm slices large diameter French bread

1/2 cup grated gruyere cheese

serves 4–6

1 Peel onions. Cut in half and slice thinly. Crush, peel and finely chop garlic.

2 Heat oil in a large saucepan and sauté onions and garlic over a medium heat until onions are golden brown.

3 Pour over hot water and crumble in stock cubes. Cover and cook for 20 minutes.

4 While soup is cooking, sprinkle cheese evenly over bread. Grill until golden. Serve soup topped with a grilled cheese crouton.

Pumpkin Soup

1kg pumpkin
1 large onion
2 cloves garlic
1 tbsp butter or oil
2 cups hot water
2 chicken stock cubes
salt
freshly ground black pepper
pinch ground nutmeg
1 cup low fat milk
chives for garnish

serves 6

1 Peel pumpkin and cut into pieces about 4cm square. Peel and roughly chop onion. Crush, peel and roughly chop garlic.

2 Melt butter or heat oil in a large saucepan. Saute onion and garlic over a moderate heat for 5 minutes or until just starting to colour.

3 Pour over hot water and crumble in stock cubes. Bring to the boil and add pumpkin. Reduce heat and simmer for 15–20 minutes, or until pumpkin is cooked.

4 Remove from heat and purée in a blender or food processor. If you have neither of these appliances, a sieve and a wooden spoon will do the job, as will a mouli or food mill.

5 Season soup with salt, pepper and nutmeg. Mix in milk and reheat to boiling. Serve garnished with chives.

Old Fashioned Vegetable Soup

1 Peel and finely chop onion. Heat oil in a saucepan. Brown meat and onion. Add bone to saucepan.

2 Pour in water and crumble in stock cube. Add split peas and barley and bring to the boil. Reduce heat and simmer for 40 minutes.

3 Wash celery and trim and slice thinly. Peel or scrub parsnip and carrot. Grate or chop finely.

4 Add vegetables to saucepan and cook for a further 15 minutes or until split peas are tender. Remove bone and meat if wished.

5 Season with freshly ground black pepper. Serve garnished with chopped parsley.

1 onion

1 tbsp oil

500g piece shin on the bone

1 1/2 litres cold water

1 beef stock cube

1/4 cup yellow split peas

2 tbsp barley

2 sticks celery

1 parsnip

1 large carrot

freshly ground black pepper

2 tbsp chopped parsley

serves 4–6

Spinach Soup

500g spinach
2 onions
2 cloves garlic
3 potatoes
25g butter
4 cups hot water
3 chicken stock cubes
pinch ground nutmeg
salt
pepper

serves 4–6

1 Wash spinach. Peel and roughly chop onions. Crush, peel and chop garlic. Peel potatoes and cut into cubes.

2 Melt butter in a large saucepan. Saute onions and garlic for 5 minutes until clear.

3 Pour in water and crumble in stock cubes. Bring to the boil and add potatoes. Cook for 10 minutes or until almost tender.

4 Add spinach and cook for a further 5 minutes. Remove from heat and purée in a blender or food processor. Season with nutmeg, salt and pepper. Serve with cheese on toast or crispy bacon.

Broccoli & Bacon Soup

1 Peel and roughly chop onion. Crush, peel and chop garlic. Derind bacon and cut flesh into small pieces.

2 Heat oil in a large saucepan and sauté onion and garlic for 5 minutes until clear.

3 Pour in water and crumble in stock cubes. Bring to the boil. Add broccoli and cook for 10 minutes until broccoli is just tender.

4 Purée in a blender or food processor. If you have neither of these appliances, a sieve and a wooden spoon will do the job, as will a mouli or food mill.

5 Return soup to saucepan. Mix in bacon and milk. Cook for 5 minutes. Season with freshly ground black pepper. Serve garnished with chives.

1 large onion
2 cloves garlic
3 rashers bacon
1 tbsp oil
3 cups hot water
3 chicken stock cubes
500g broccoli
freshly ground black pepper
1 cup low fat milk
chives for garnish

serves 4

Prawn Chowder

2 large onions
2 cloves garlic
2 large potatoes
25g butter
3 tbsp plain flour
4 cups hot water
2 chicken stock cubes
sprig parsley
1 bay leaf
sprig thyme
2 cups milk
200g can small prawns
freshly ground black pepper
½ tsp salt
2 tbsp chopped parsley

serves 4

1 Peel onions and chop finely. Crush, peel and chop garlic. Peel potatoes and cut into 1½ cm cubes.

2 Melt butter in a large saucepan. Saute onion and garlic for 5 minutes or until clear. Stir in flour. Add potatoes, water and crumbled stock cubes.

3 Tie parsley, bay leaf and thyme together with a piece of thread to make a bouquet garni. Add to saucepan. Bring to the boil and cook for 10 minutes or until potatoes are soft.

4 Add milk and prawns. Bring to the boil. Remove bouquet garni. Season with freshly ground black pepper and salt. Garnish with chopped parsley.

Mussel Soup

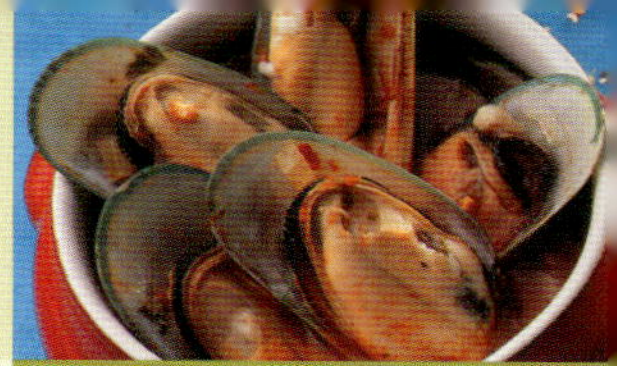

1 Scrub and debeard the mussels. Crush, peel and finely chop garlic. Peel and chop onion.

2 Heat oil in a large saucepan. Add onion and garlic and cook until clear. Add parsley and chilli and cook for 1–2 minutes. Increase heat and add lemon juice, wine and water and bring to the boil.

3 Remove seeds and core from tomatoes and chop flesh. Add tomato flesh and juice to the saucepan. Bring to the boil.

4 Add mussels and cook covered over a moderate heat for about 5 minutes. Discard any mussels that do not open. Remove the top shell from the mussels.

5 Season to taste with salt and freshly ground black pepper and serve immediately.

30 fresh mussels
2 cloves garlic
1 onion
2 tbsp light olive oil
2 tbsp chopped parsley
1 tsp chopped chilli
2 tbsp lemon juice
3/4 cup dry white wine
1 1/2 cups water
400g can tomatoes in juice
salt
freshly ground black pepper

serves 4–6

Carrot & Coriander Soup

500g carrots
2 large onions
2 cloves garlic
1 tbsp butter
1/4 cup sherry
2 chicken stock cubes
4 cups hot water
8 sprigs fresh coriander
freshly ground black pepper

serves 4

1 Scrub or peel carrots. Cut into 3cm lengths. Peel and roughly chop onions. Crush, peel and chop garlic.

2 Melt butter in a large saucepan. Saute onion and garlic over a low heat for about 5 minutes or until clear.

3 Add sherry to saucepan and crumble in stock cubes. Pour in hot water and bring to the boil. Add carrots. Cook for 20 minutes, or until carrots are tender.

4 Puree in a blender or food processor with the coriander. Season with freshly ground black pepper.

Curried Lentil Soup

1 cup brown lentils
1 large onion
2 cloves garlic
1 tbsp oil
1 tbsp curry powder
7 cups hot water
310g can tomato purée
4 beef stock cubes

serves 4–6

1 Wash lentils, cover with cold water and soak while preparing remaining ingredients.

2 Peel onion and finely chop. Crush, peel and chop garlic. Heat oil in a large saucepan and sauté onion and garlic for 5 minutes or until onion is clear.

3 Add curry powder and cook for 1 minute or until curry smells fragrant.

4 Add hot water, tomato purée, crumbled stock cubes and lentils to saucepan. Cover and cook for 1–1 1/4 hours or until lentils are tender. Serve with a salad and crusty French bread.

Quick Malaysian Chicken Soup

2 cloves garlic
2cm piece root ginger
1 onion
1 carrot
1 stick celery
1 tbsp oil
1 to 2 cups chopped cooked or uncooked fresh chicken
3 cups hot water
2 chicken stock cubes
400g can tomatoes in juice
1 tbsp sweet chilli sauce
1/4 cup coconut cream
400g packet instant noodles
chopped parsley

serves 4

1 Crush, peel and chop garlic. Peel ginger and finely chop. Peel onion and carrot and cut into 1cm cubes. Wash and trim celery. Cut into 1cm slices.

2 Heat oil in a large saucepan or flameproof clay pot. Saute garlic, ginger, onion, carrot and celery for 5 minutes or until onion is clear.

3 Add chicken, water, crumbled chicken stock cubes, tomatoes in juice, chilli sauce and coconut cream. Break tomatoes up with a wooden spoon.

4 Bring to the boil. Reduce heat and simmer for 10 minutes. Add noodles and cook for 2–3 minutes or until noodles are cooked. Serve garnished with chopped parsley.

Avocado Summer Soup & Chilled Melon and Cucumber Soup

Avocado Summer Soup

1 Chop avocado flesh and purée in food processor or blender.

2 While motor is running add stock, wine, cream, and lemon juice. Blend until smooth.

3 Chill soup until ready to serve. Garnish with red capsicum and dill sprigs.

serves 6

4 ripe avocados, peeled and stoned

500mL chicken stock

125mL dry white wine

60mL double cream

3 tbsp lemon juice

red capsicum strips and dill sprigs for garnish

Chilled Melon and Cucumber Soup

1 In a food processor or blender, purée melon and cucumbers until smooth; strain.

2 Add honey and lemon juice; pour mixture into jug, cover and set aside. Roughly chop mint (reserve some for garnish) and mix into puréed mixture. Let mixture stand for 5 hours at room temperature.

4 Remove chopped mint from soup, chill until ready to garnish and serve.

1 cantaloupe melon, peeled and seeded

4 cucumbers, peeled and seeded

2 tbsp honey

2 tbsp lemon juice

8–12 mint sprigs

serves 6 makes 12

Cream of Squash Soup & Coriander Yoghurt Soup

15g butter & 1 onion, chopped

500g yellow squash, chopped

500mL chicken stock & 250mL soured cream

pinch nutmeg & salt

freshly ground black pepper

2 tbsp soured cream and snipped chives for garnish

serves 4

Cream of Squash Soup

1 Melt butter in a large saucepan, add squash and onion, cook until squash is cooked through. Add stock to mixture, bring to the boil and simmer for 20 minutes, or until squash falls apart.

2 Remove from heat and purée until smooth. Transfer mixture to a large saucepan, mix in cream and nutmeg, season. Reheat, garnish and serve.

600mL natural yoghurt

90g fresh coriander, chopped

½ onion, finely chopped

250mL single cream

750mL chicken stock

parsley sprig for garnish

serves 6

Coriander Yoghurt Soup

1 In a food processor or blender, purée yoghurt, coriander, onion and cream until smooth.

2 Pour into a large container, add stock, mix well. Chill until ready to serve. Garnish with parsley.

Wood-Roasted Salmon & Potato Soup

1 onion

2 cloves garlic

25g butter

6 cups chicken stock

4 large potatoes

2 tsp grated lemon rind

200g wood-roasted smoked salmon

fresh chives

serves 4–6

1 Peel onion and chop finely. Crush, peel and chop garlic. Melt butter in a large saucepan and sauté onion and garlic for 5 minutes.

2 Add chicken stock and bring to the boil. Peel potatoes and cut into 1cm cubes. Add to stock with thyme. Cover and simmer for 10 minutes or until potatotes are cooked.

3 Mix in lemon rind. Remove skin from smoked salmon and break flesh into chunks. Mix into soup. Bring to the boil and serve garnished with chives.

Fish & Rice Soup

1 onion

1 clove garlic

25g butter

6 cups fish stock

1 cup long grain rice

200g mixed fish sauce as prawns, scallops, mussels and white flesh fish fillets

1 cup unsweetened natural yoghurt

2 tbsp chopped parsley

serves 4

1 Peel onion and chop finely. Crush, peel and chop garlic.

2 Melt butter and sauté onion and garlic until onion is clear. Add fish stock and bring to the boil. Add rice. Cover and cook for 7 minutes.

3 Prepare fish as necessary, cutting fillets into cubes. Add to soup and cook for 4 minutes or until rice and fish are cooked.

4 Stir in yoghurt. Bring to the boil but do not boil. Mix in parsley and serve.

Roasted Tomato & Fish Soup

1 Cut tomatoes in half and place cut side down in a roasting dish. Peel onions, cut into quarters and place around tomatoes. Cut capsicum in half, deseed and add to baking dish.

2 Drizzle oil over. Bake at 200°C for 15 minutes or until skins break from tomatoes.

3 Remove tomato skins. Place tomatoes, onions and capsicum in a food processor or blender and process until smooth.

4 Place in a saucepan with stock, sugar and salt. Cut fish into 2cm cubes. Add to saucepan. Bring to the boil and simmer for 5 minutes or until fish is just cooked.

5 Spread bread with pesto. Cut into quarters and grill until golden on both sides. Serve soup with pesto croutons and torn basil leaves.

2kg tomatoes

2 onions

2 red capsicum

3 tbsp chilli oil

2 cups fish stock

1 tsp sugar

1 tsp salt

2 skinned and boned fish fillets

6 x 2cm-thick slices stale French bread

1/4 cup basil pesto

basil leaves to garnish

serves 6

Smoked Fish Chowder

3 large onions
3 cloves garlic
2 large potatoes
25g butter
4 cups fish stock
1 bouquet garni
3 tbsp plain flour
2 cups low-fat milk
250g smoked fish
salt and pepper
2 tbsp chopped parsley
¼ cup low-fat sour cream

serves 4–6

1 Peel onions and chop finely. Crush, peel and chop garlic. Peel potatoes and cut into cubes.

2 Melt butter and sauté onion and garlic for 5 minutes or until clear.

3 Add fish stock and bouquet garni and bring to the boil. Add potatoes. Cook for 10 minutes or until potatoes are tender.

4 Mix flour with a little of the milk to make a smooth paste. Stir into stock mixture with milk and smoked fish. Bring to the boil, stirring.

5 Season with salt and pepper and add parsley. Serve piping hot garnished with sour cream.

Thai Prawn Soup

6 cups chicken stock

1 tsp finely chopped lemon grass

1 tbsp finely chopped fresh ginger

1 tbsp lemon juice

1/2 to 1 tsp prepared minced chilli

4 kaffir lime leaves

1 tbsp Thai fish sauce

12 shelled uncooked prawns

1 tbsp chopped fresh coriander

serves 4

1 Bring chicken stock, lemon grass, ginger, lemon juice, minced chilli, lime leaves and fish sauce to the boil. Simmer for 2 minutes.

2 Add prawns and cook for 3 minutes or until prawns are just cooked. Garnish with coriander leaves and serve immediately.

Mixed Mushroom Noodle Soup

30g dried shitake mushrooms

1 litre reduced salt vegetable stock

3cm piece ginger, crushed

1 halved garlic clove

1 whole star anise

1 tbsp reduced salt soy sauce

100g oyster mushrooms

400g fresh udon noodles

3 spring onions, sliced

100g enoki mushrooms, gently separated

serves 6

1 Put the shitake mushrooms in an ovenproof bowl, add 1 cup boiling water and allow to stand for 25 minutes or until the mushrooms are soft. Drian, then strain and reserve the liquid. Cut the mushrooms into thin slices.

2 Put the stock, mushroom liquid, ginger, garlic, star anise and soy into a large pot and bring to the boil. Reduce the heat and simmer for 10 minutes. Remove the ginger, garlic and star anise and discard.

3 Add the oyster mushrooms, dried shitake, udon noodles and spring onions and simmer gently for 5 minutes.

4 Stir in the enoki and heat for 1 minute or until they soften. Serve hot.

Dutch Country Cheese Soup

1 Melt the butter and oil in large saucepan until foaming. Add the onion and celery and sauté for 5 minutes until the vegetables are golden. Add the diced potatoes, pieces of cauliflower and carrots and continue to sauté for 5 minutes until golden.

2 Add the stock and bring the soup to the boil. Simmer for 30 minutes until all the vegetables are tender. Season to taste with salt and pepper.

3 Add 200g of the gouda and stir gently to distribute.

4 Grill the bread slices on both sides then top with grated cheese. Grill until the cheese melts.

5 Ladle the soup into deep bowls then top with a hot slice of the grilled cheese bread.

6 Sprinkle with the chervil (or parsley) and serve immediately.

2 tbsp butter

1 tbsp olive oil

1 large onion, chopped

4 stalks celery, sliced

1kg white potatoes, peeled and diced

1 small head of cauliflower, trimmed and cut into florets

400g carrots, peeled and chopped

7–8 cups vegetable stock

salt and pepper, to taste

400g gouda cheese, wax removed, grated

6 slices country-style loaf or baguette

2 tbsp chopped chervil or parsley

serves 6

Summer Garden Tomato Soup

- 1 tbsp olive oil
- 2 shallots
- 1 large Spanish onion, chopped
- 2 cloves garlic, minced
- 2 large sprigs thyme
- 1 1/2 kg summer tomatoes, either red or yellow, roughly chopped
- 2 tbsp tomato paste (omit if using yellow tomatoes)
- 2 cups vegetable stock
- 1 tbsp sugar
- salt and pepper to taste
- 2 punnets assorted tiny tomatoes, chopped (optional)
- 1 bunch basil
- 150g fetta cheese, finely crumbled

1 Heat the olive oil and sauté the chopped shallots, Spanish onion, garlic and thyme until softened. Add the chopped tomatoes and tomato paste and sauté for a further 2 minutes.

2 Add the vegetable stock, sugar and salt and pepper to taste and bring to the boil. Simmer for 25 minutes then purée with a hand-held 'wand' or in a food processor. The soup should be thick enough to support the garnish. If it seems a little thin, simmer for a further 10 minutes to reduce.

3 Meanwhile, prepare the garnish. Quarter all the tiny tomatoes (if using) and finely slice the basil leaves with a very sharp knife. In a separate bowl, crumble the fetta cheese and set aside.

4 To serve the soup, divide into deep bowls then heavily garnish with a pile of chopped tomatoes, basil leaves and fetta cheese.

Meatballs in Egg and Lemon Soup *Youvarlakia*

500g beef mince
1 medium onion, minced
1/4 cup parsley, chopped
1/4 cup short grain rice
1 egg
salt and pepper
1/3 cup cornflour
1 litre beef stock
50g butter
1 egg
75mL lemon juice

serves 6

1 Combine the mince, onions, parsley, rice and egg in a bowl, and mix well with your hands. Season well with salt and pepper. Using one tablespoon of mixture for each meatball, shape mixture into balls, and roll in cornflour (shaking off the excess).

2 Bring the stock and the butter to the boil, then reduce the heat and place the meatballs in the stock. Cover with a lid, and simmer for 45 minutes (until they are cooked). Let cool slightly.

3 Whisk the egg and lemon juice together in a bowl, then add 100mL of warm stock to the egg and lemon juice. Pour this mixture back into the saucepan and heat very gently.

4 Season with salt and pepper before serving.

Chickpea, Roasted Tomato and Garlic Soup

500g dried chickpeas
1kg roma tomatoes
1 bulb garlic
85mL olive oil
salt
2 tbsp dried oregano
2 leeks, sliced, white part only
1 litre chicken stock
2 tbsp tomato paste
salt and pepper
oregano leaves, fresh

serves 4

1 Soak chickpeas in cold water overnight. Place chickpeas in a saucepan covered with water and bring to the boil, then simmer for approximately one hour until chick peas are cooked. Drain and set aside.

2 Pre-heat the oven to 200°C. Halve the tomatoes and place them in a baking tray. Cut the top off the garlic bulb and place in the baking tray. Drizzle with olive oil, sprinkle with salt and dried oregano, and roast in the oven for 20–30 minutes.

3 Place the tomatoes and five peeled garlic cloves (reserve the rest) in a food processor, and purée for one minute.

4 Heat half the oil and sauté the leeks for three minutes. Add the stock, and bring to the boil, then reduce heat to simmer. Add the tomato mixture, tomato paste and the chickpeas, season with salt and pepper, and heat through.

5 To serve, sprinkle with fresh oregano leaves just before serving.

Mixed Bean and Vegetable Soup

1/2 cup haricot beans, soaked overnight

1/2 cup chick peas, soaked overnight

3 tbsp olive oil

1 medium onion, diced & 1 clove garlic, crushed

1 leek, white part only, diced

1 1/2 litres vegetable stock

2 sticks celery, sliced & 1 carrot, diced

2 sprigs fresh thyme, chopped

1 small fennel bulb, grated

2 zucchinis, grated

90g broad beans

3 medium tomatoe, peeled, seeded and chopped

salt and freshly ground black pepper

freshly grated Parmesan, for serving.

1 Drain the haricot beans and chick peas. Place in a saucepan, cover with water and bring to the boil for 15 minutes. Cover and simmer for a further 30 minutes before draining again.

2 Heat the oil in a saucepan and add the onion, garlic and leek. Continue stirring until tender. Add the stock, haricot beans and chickpeas. Cover, and simmer for 45 minutes (until tender). Add the remaining ingredients and simmer for a further 15 minutes.

3 Taste for seasoning, and serve with freshly grated Parmesan.

serves 4-6

Chilled Yoghurt Soup

1 large telegraph cucumber

250mL light single cream

200mL natural yoghurt

2 tbsp white wine vinegar

1 tbsp balsamic vinegar

2 tbsp fresh mint, chopped

1 clove garlic, crushed

salt and freshly ground black pepper

extra mint and slices of cucumber, to garnish.

serves 4–6

1 Peel and grate the cucumber.

2 Combine the cream, yoghurt and vinegars together, and whisk lightly, until smooth. Stir in the cucumber, mint, garlic and seasoning. Cover and chill for three hours.

3 Stir and taste for seasoning before serving chilled. Garnish with a slice of cucumber, a sprig of mint and cracked pepper.

Thai Broth with Chicken and Vegetables

1 stalk lemon grass

1 1/5 litres chicken stock

4 tbsp Thai fish sauce

1 tbsp caster sugar

1 red chilli, deseeded and sliced

1 clove garlic, sliced

2 1/2 cm piece fresh root ginger, thinly sliced

3 skinless boneless chicken breasts, thinly sliced

1 carrot, cut into matchsticks

1 stick celery, sliced

4 spring onions, sliced, plus 1 spring onion, shredded, to garnish

juice of 1 lime

1 tbsp each of roughly chopped fresh coriander, mint and basil

1 Peel the outer covering from the lemon grass stalk, then finely chop the lower white bulbous part and discard the fibrous top.

2 Place the stock, fish sauce, sugar, lemon grass, chilli, garlic and ginger in a saucepan. Bring to the boil, then reduce the heat and simmer, covered, for 10 minutes to release their flavours.

3 Add the chicken slices to the broth and cook for 2 minutes, then add the carrot, celery and spring onions and cook for a further 5 minutes or until the vegetables and chicken are cooked and tender. Add the lime juice and herbs to the broth and heat through. Garnish with the shredded spring onion.

serves 4

Curried Sweet Potato Soup

2 tsp canola oil

1/2 carrot, 1/2 onion & 1 stalk celery diced

1 clove garlic, crushed

2 tsp curry powder & 1/2 tsp cumin seeds

1/2 tsp yellow mustard seeds

2 tbsp chopped fresh coriander

4 cups low-salt vegetable stock

1/2 cup beer or stout & 1 tbsp honey

455g orange sweet potato, chopped & 1/2 tsp ground cinnamon

1 sugar banana, chopped (optional)

lime wedges to serve

Lime Yoghurt

1/2 cup low-fat natural yoghurt

2 tsp finely grated lime zest

2 tsp lime juice

1 Heat the oil in a saucepan over a medium heat. Add the carrot, onion, celery and garlic. Cook, stirring, for 3 minutes. Stir in curry powder and cumin and mustard seeds. Cook until the mustard seeds start to pop.

2 Add the coriander, stock, beer and honey. Bring to the boil. Add the sweet potato, cinnamon and banana (if using). Simmer, stirring occasionally, until the sweet potato is soft. Cool slightly.

3 Transfer the mixture to a food processor or blender. Purée in batches. Return the mixture to a clean saucepan. Reheat.

4 To make the lime yoghurt Place the yoghurt and lime zest and juice in a small bowl. Mix to combine.

5 To serve, ladle the soup into warm bowls. Top with a spoonful of Lime Yoghurt. Serve with lime wedges.

The banana creates a unique flavour – one that you may or may not. The soup is still divine without it.

serves 6

German Potato Soup with Cauliflower and Caraway

1 Cut 5cm lengths off the end of each spring onion. Using a sharp knife, slice these into thin strips, keeping one end intact to hold the strips together. Plunge the strips into a bowl of icy water and set aside until they curl, about 1 hour.

2 Heat the olive oil in a large saucepan and add the remaining spring onions, sliced diagonally, and sauté for a moment or two. Add the cauliflower florets, potatoes and caraway seeds and sauté for 10 minutes until golden.

3 Add the stock and bring the soup to the boil. Simmer for 45 minutes then process in a food processor (or with a hand-held 'wand') until smooth.

4 Add the reserved small cauliflower florets and simmer for 10 minutes.

5 Serve the soup drizzled with a little yoghurt, a sprinkling of caraway and the spring onion curls.

1 bunch spring onions, sliced

2 tbsp olive oil

1 medium cauliflower head, cut into florets (reserve small florets)

570g white potatoes, peeled and diced

1 tsp caraway seeds

6 cups vegetable stock

2 tbsp mild yoghurt

extra sprinkling of caraway seeds

serves 6

Indian Curried Vegetable Soup

2 tbsp butter or ghee
2 tsp turmeric
4 cloves garlic, minced
1 tbsp mild curry powder & 1 tbsp garam masala
1 tbsp ground ginger & 1 tsp chilli flakes
4 medium potatoes & 2 sweet potatoes (kumera)
2 turnips & 1 parsnip
4 medium carrots
1 medium butternut pumpkin
4 medium zucchini
400g peas, shelled
4 cups vegetable stock
400mL coconut milk
salt and pepper
1 cup coriander leaves to garnish

1 Heat the butter or ghee and add the turmeric, garlic, curry powder, garam masala, ginger and chilli flakes and sauté the ingredients until the spices are fragrant.

2 Meanwhile, peel and chop all the root vegetables and the pumpkin. Slice the zucchini and shell the peas.

3 Add the chopped vegetables (not the zucchini and peas) to the spice mixture and add the stock and bring the soup to the boil. Simmer for 45 minutes until the vegetables are very soft.

4 Add the coconut milk, zucchini and peas and continue to simmer for 15 minutes. Season with salt and pepper and serve, garnished with coriander and accompanied by toasted Indian bread and cucumber yoghurt.

serves 4

Portuguese Potato and Bean Soup

- *4 cloves garlic*
- *2 medium onions*
- *2 medium carrots*
- *4 medium potatoes*
- *1 green capsicum*
- *425g can Italian tomatoes, chopped*
- *1/2 medium green cabbage, sliced*
- *425g can kidney beans, drained and rinsed*
- *455g smoked Polish sausage, diced*
- *6 1/2 cups chicken stock*
- *salt and pepper*
- *2 tbsp chopped parsley to garnish*

serves 6–8

1 Peel and mince the garlic, peel and dice the onions, carrots and potatoes. Finely dice the capsicum and tomatoes.

2 Place all the ingredients into a large pot and bring to the boil. Reduce the heat to a simmer and partially cover with a lid.

3 Simmer for 2 hours, stirring occasionally. After 2 hours, add salt and pepper to taste and serve piping hot, garnished with parsley.

You will love the flavours in this satisfying and full-flavoured soup. It is incredibly quick and easy to prepare and makes a perfect Sunday night supper soup. Since this soup contains no oil, you can make this a regular, guilt-free indulgence.

Potato Bacon Chowder

225g bacon, chopped
30g butter
2 large onions, chopped
4 stalks celery, chopped
2 tsp dried thyme
2 tbsp plain flour
6 cups chicken stock
2 large potatoes, peeled and cubed
285mL sour cream
3 tbsp chopped fresh parsley
2 tbsp snipped fresh chives

makes 6

1 Place the bacon in a large, heavy-based saucepan and cook over a medium heat for 5 minutes or until golden and crisp. Remove from the pan and drain on absorbent kitchen paper.

2 Melt the butter in the pan and cook the onions, celery and thyme over a low heat for 4–5 minutes or until onion is soft.

3 Return the bacon to the pan, then stir in the flour and cook for 1 minute. Remove the pan from the heat and gradually blend in the stock. Bring to the boil, then reduce the heat. Add the potatoes and cook for 10 minutes or until they're tender.

4 Remove pan from heat and stir in the sour cream and parsley. Return to the heat and cook without boiling, stirring constantly, for 1–2 minutes. Ladle soup the into bowls, sprinkle with chives and serve immediately.

Sweet Potato and Rosemary Soup

40mL olive oil
2 cloves garlic, crushed
1 medium onion, chopped
1 tbsp rosemary, chopped
2 tbsp tomato pesto
1 medium carrot, diced
1 large potato, diced
680g sweet potato, diced
4 cups chicken stock
freshly ground pepper and salt
2 tbsp rosemary, chopped, extra

serves 4–6

1 Heat the oil in a saucepan, add the garlic, onion and rosemary, and cook on medium heat for 3–5 minutes, or until soft.

2 Add the tomato pesto and cook, for 1 minute.

3 Add the carrot, potato and sweet potato, and cook a further 5 minutes. Add the chicken stock and pepper and salt, bring to boil, reduce the heat, and simmer (with the lid on) for 30–40 minutes, or until vegetables are soft.

4 Purée the soup in a food processor (you may have to do this in two batches), return the soup to pan, add the rosemary and heat through before serving. Add extra stock if soup is too thick.

Avocado Gazpazho

2 large ripe avocados, stoned, peeled and chopped

grated zest and juice of 1 lemon

$2^1/_2$ cups vegetable stock

2 large tomatoes

1 cucumber, chopped

1 green and 1 red capsicum, deseeded and chopped

1 clove garlic, crushed

salt and black pepper

4 tbsp freshly snipped chives to garnish

serves 4

1 Place the avocados, lemon zest and juice and the stock in a food processor and blend to a thin, smooth purée, or use a hand blender. Pour into a large bowl and set aside.

2 Place the tomatoes in a bowl, cover with boiling water and leave for 30 seconds. Remove from the bowl, peel off the skins, then deseed and chop the flesh. Reserve a little chopped tomato and cucumber to garnish. Place the rest of the tomatoes and cucumber in the food processor with the capsicum, garlic and seasoning, then blend to a purée. Alternatively, use a hand blender.

3 Add the tomato mixture to the avocado purée, mixing thoroughly. Cover and refrigerate for 1 hour, then serve garnished with chives and the reserved tomato and cucumber.

On a balmy summer evening, what better start to a meal than this iced gazpacho with its extra avocado? Serve with crusty bread to mop up the last delicious drop!

French Vegetable Soup with Pistou

1 If using dried beans, soak overnight.

2 Place the soaked and drained dried beans in a pan with fresh water to cover. Bring to the boil, cover and simmer gently for 15 minutes. Drain.

3 Chop the onion finely. Trim and cut the zucchini or squash into 5mm slices. Peel the potatoes and cut into 1cm dice.

4 Melt the butter in a large deep pan and sauté the prepared vegetables, including the dried and cooked, or fresh white beans, until softened for about 5 minutes. Cover with cold water and add salt. Cover and simmer gently for 1 hour. Add the farfalle to the soup, cooking for a further 15 minutes.

5 Make pistou by processing the basil with the garlic in a food processor or blender. Peel and chop the tomato and add to the basil with the tomato paste and cheese. Purée to a paste, adding oil gradually.

6 Stir the pistou into the soup just before serving. Serve piping hot with crusty bread.

455g fresh borlotti or dried navy beans & 1 large onion

455g green beans

455g zucchini or squash

6 medium potatoes, 30g butter & 14 cups water

1–2 tsp salt (the amount of vegetables calls for a good seasoning)

55g farfalle (pasta bows)

Pistou

1 cup basil leaves

4 cloves garlic

1 large tomato

1 tbs tomato paste

1/2 cup grated Parmesan or Gruyere cheese

3 tbs olive oil

serves 4–6

Spinach and Almond Soup

455g baby spinach
3 1/2 cups vegetable stock
100g ground almonds
salt and black pepper
115mL single cream
55g Parmesan, grated, to serve

serves 4

1 Put the spinach into a large saucepan with the stock, reserving a few leaves to garnish. Bring to the boil, then reduce the heat and simmer for 5 minutes. Stir in the almonds and seasoning and simmer for 2 minutes. Remove from the heat and leave to cool a little.

2 Pour into a food processor and blend to a smooth purée, or use a hand blender. Add the cream, return to the pan and reheat gently - don't let the soup boil. Serve topped with the Parmesan and a sprinkling of pepper, and garnished with the reserved spinach.

Not only do the almonds add their distinctive taste to this spinach soup, they also give it a lovely thick texture. It's delicious hot or cold - especially if you use fresh stock.

Tuscan Bean and Bread Soup

½ loaf ciabatta bread
3 tbsp olive oil
3 onions, chopped
3 cloves garlic, chopped
2 x 400g cans chopped tomatoes
400g can flageolet beans
2½ cups vegetable stock
salt and black pepper
fresh basil to garnish

Oven temperature 150°C

serves 4

1 Preheat the oven. Cut the ciabatta into dice, then place in the oven for 10 minutes to dry out.

2 Heat the oil in a large saucepan, add the onions and garlic, and cook for 3–4 minutes, until soft. Add the tomatoes, beans and stock, bring to the boil, then simmer for 2 minutes.

3 Stir in the diced ciabatta, bring the soup back to the boil, then simmer for a further 5 minutes. Season, then serve garnished with basil.

Leek, Lime and Coconut Soup

- *2 tbsp olive oil*
- *3 leeks, thinly sliced*
- *1 green chilli, deseeded and chopped*
- *2 potatoes, diced*
- *grated zest and juice of 2 limes, plus a few extra slices to garnish*
- *salt and black pepper*
- *$2^{1}/_{4}$ cups vegetable stock*
- *1 cup coconut milk*
- *fresh coriander to garnish*

serves 4

1 Heat the oil in a large heavy-based saucepan, then add the leeks, chilli, potatoes, lime zest and seasoning. Cook for 2 minutes, then add the stock and bring to the boil. Reduce the heat and simmer for 20–25 minutes, until the potatoes are tender. Leave to cool slightly.

2 Transfer the soup to a food processor and blend briefly to make a chunky, creamy mixture, or use a hand blender. Return the soup to the pan.

3 Stir in the lime juice, then add the coconut milk and heat through, taking care not to let the soup boil. Serve hot or cold, garnished with slices of lime and the coriander.

The Thai flavours of lime and coconut totally transform this classic leek and potato soup. You can enjoy it hot or cold, depending on your mood and the weather.

Thick Minestrone with Pesto

3 tbsp olive oil
1 onion, chopped
2 cloves garlic, chopped
1 potato, cut into 1cm cubes
2 small carrots, cut into 1cm cubes
1 large zucchini, cut into 1cm cubes
1/4 white cabbage, chopped
3 cups vegetable stock
2 x 400g cans chopped tomatoes
85g pasta shapes, such as conchiglie shells
salt and black pepper
4 tbsp grated Parmesan
4 tbsp pesto

serves 4

1 Place the oil in a large heavy-based saucepan, then add the onion, garlic, potato, carrots, zucchini and cabbage and cook for 5–7 minutes, until slightly softened.

2 Add the stock and tomatoes and bring to the boil. Reduce the heat and simmer for 20 minutes, then add the pasta and seasoning and cook for a further 15 minutes or until the pasta is tender but still firm to the bite. Divide the soup between bowls and top each serving with a tablespoon of Parmesan and pesto.

Curried Cream of Vegetable Soup

3 tbsp groundnut or vegetable oil

2 tbsp curry powder

pinch each of ground cinnamon, nutmeg, turmeric and ginger

3 carrots, diced

2 onions & 2 cloves garlic, chopped

2 potatoes & 2 zucchinis, diced

4 cups vegetable stock

285g can cannellini beans, drained

225g can red kidney beans, drained

200mL crème fraîche

salt

2 tsp chopped fresh Italian parsley to garnish

1 Place the oil in a large heavy-based saucepan. Add the curry powder, cinnamon, nutmeg, turmeric and ginger and cook for 1 minute, then add the carrots, onions, garlic, potatoes and zucchinis. Stir to coat thoroughly in the oil and spice mixture and cook for a further 5 minutes.

2 Add the stock and bring to the boil. Reduce the heat and simmer for 20 minutes or until the vegetables are tender. Add the cannellini and red kidney beans and gently heat through. Remove from the heat and stir in the crème fraîche. Season to taste and serve sprinkled with the parsley.

A dollop of crème fraîche makes a creamy contrast to the spicy flavour of this versatile soup. Use seasonal vegetables, and serve with warm French bread.

serves 4

Plum Tomato, Lentil and Basil Soup

1 Rinse the lentils, drain, then add them to a large saucepan of boiling water. Simmer, covered, for 25 minutes or until tender. Drain, rinse and set aside.

2 Meanwhile, place the tomatoes in a bowl, cover with boiling water, leave for 30 seconds, then drain. Remove the skins, deseed and chop. Heat the oil in a large saucepan, add the onions and cook for 10 minutes or until softened, stirring occasionally. Stir in the tomatoes, tomato purée, stock, bay leaf, and pepper. Bring to the boil and simmer, covered, stirring occasionally, for 25 minutes or until all the vegetables are cooked.

3 Remove the pan from the heat and cool for a few minutes. Remove and discard the bay leaf, then purée the soup until smooth in a food processor, liquidizer, or with a hand blender. Return to a clean pan, stir in the lentils and chopped basil, then reheat gently. Serve garnished with the fresh basil.

6 tbsp continental lentils

910g plum tomatoes

1 tbsp olive oil

2 onions, chopped

2 tbsp sun-dried tomato purée

3 cups vegetable stock

1 bay leaf

black pepper

3 tbsp chopped fresh basil, plus extra leaves to garnish

serves 4

Watercress Soup

1 tbsp sunflower oil
4 scallions, finely chopped
1 leek, thinly sliced
225g potatoes, diced
1 cup watercress, chopped
2 cups vegetable stock
2 cups half-fat milk
black pepper

serves 4

1 Heat the oil in a large saucepan, then add the scallions and leek and cook gently for 5 minutes or until softened, stirring occasionally. Add the potatoes and watercress to the scallion mixture and cook for a further 3 minutes or until the watercress wilts, stirring occasionally.

2 Stir in the stock, milk and pepper. Bring to a boil, then reduce the heat and simmer, covered, for 20 minutes or until the potatoes are cooked and tender, stirring occasionally.

3 Remove the pan from the heat and cool for a few minutes. Purée the soup until smooth in a food processor, liquidizer, or with a hand blender. Return to a clean pan and reheat gently, until piping hot. Serve seasoned with the coarsely ground black pepper.

This quick soup is full of goodness but it looks and tastes sophisticated enough to serve up at any dinner party. For a change, use chopped spinach instead of watercress.

Cumin-Spiced Carrot Soup

1 tbsp olive oil
1 large onion, chopped
1 clove garlic, crushed
3 sticks celery, chopped
1 tbsp ground cumin
680g carrots, thinly sliced
4 cups vegetable stock
black pepper
fresh coriander to garnish

serves 4

1 Heat the oil in a large saucepan. Add the onion, garlic, and celery and fry gently for 5 minutes or until softened, stirring occasionally. Add the cumin and fry, stirring, for 1 minute to release its flavour.

2 Add the carrots, stock and pepper to the onion mixture and stir to combine. Bring to the boil and simmer, covered, for 30–35 minutes, until the vegetables are tender, stirring occasionally.

3 Remove the pan from the heat and cool for a few minutes. Purée the soup until smooth in a food processor, liquidizer, or with a hand blender. Return to a clean pan and reheat gently. Serve garnished with the fresh coriander.

This thick soup, will really warm you up on a cold winter's night. To get the best flavour, spend a bit extra on fresh stock. Serve with naan bread.

Mixed Vegetable and Bean Soup

- *2 tbsp olive oil*
- *1 onion, finely chopped*
- *2 cloves garlic, crushed*
- *1 potato, 1 carrot, finely diced*
- *2 tsp cumin seeds*
- *4 cups vegetable bouillon*
- *2 sticks celery, finely chopped*
- *1 large zucchini, finely chopped*
- *115 g green beans, cut into $2^{1}/_{2}$ cm pieces*
- *400g can wax beans, drained*
- *400g can chopped tomatoes*
- *freshly ground black pepper*
- *55g Cheddar cheese, grated*

serves 4

1 Heat the oil in a large heavy-based saucepan, then add the onion, garlic, potato, carrot and cumin seeds. Cook, uncovered, for 5 minutes, stirring from time to time, until the vegetables have softened.

2 Add the bouillon, celery and zucchini and bring to the boil. Cover and simmer for 10 minutes or until the celery and zucchini are tender.

3 Stir in the green beans, wax beans, tomatoes and plenty of pepper. Simmer, uncovered, for 5 minutes or until the green beans are tender. Pour the soup into bowls and top with the Cheddar.

Cumin adds a touch of spice to this chunky soup topped with cheese. Use your favorite vegetables, but cut them into even-sized pieces so they cook in the same time.

Minted Pea and Potato Soup

4 potatoes (about 455 g), peeled and chopped

4 cups reduced salt chicken bouillon

1 bay leaf

455 g frozen baby mint peas

2 large sprigs basil

4 tbsp reduced fat sour cream

cracked black pepper to taste

serves 6

1 Put the potatoes and bouillon in a large pot and bring to the boil. Add the bay leaf and simmer over a medium heat for 15 minutes or until the potatoes are just tender.

2 Add the peas and basil and simmer for 5 minutes or until the peas are tender. Take care not to overcook or the peas will lose their rich color. Remove the bay leaf and basil and discard.

3 In a food processor, process the soup in batches until smooth, then return to the pot and reheat gently.

4 Ladle the soup into bowls and put a spoonful of sour cream in the center of each. Stir gently with a skewer to make a swirl pattern in the top of the soup and season with pepper.

Clam and Black Mussel Broth

45mL vegetable oil

1 onion finely chopped

2 tbsp Tom Yum paste

200 g surf clams, cleaned and sand-less

200 g black mussels, cleaned

2 cups chicken stock

1 stalk lemon grass, chopped

juice of one lime

1 tbsp coriander stalk and roots, finely chopped

1 tbsp Thai fish sauce

1 tbsp fresh coriander leaves roughly chopped

serves 6

1 Heat the oil in a wok or large cooking pot. Add the onion, Tom Yum paste, clams and mussels. Simmer, covered with a lid, for 30 seconds.

2 Add chicken stock, lemon grass, lime juice, coriander stalk and roots, Thai fish sauce and stir through. Cook until all the shells have opened.

3 Add the fresh coriander leaves and serve in soup bowls.

Garlic Soup

1 In a large saucepan, combine broth, bones, garlic head, parsley and salt and pepper. Bring to the boil, reduce heat to medium and simmer, uncovered, for 30 minutes. Strain into another saucepan.

2 Meanwhile, heat 1 tbsp oil in a medium skillet and sauté chopped garlic over medium heat until lightly golden. Add ham and cook for 1 minute. Stir in paprika and cumin and remove immediately from heat. Add the garlic mixture to the soup and simmer.

3 Preheat the oven to 180°C. Arrange bread slices on a baking sheet and brush lightly with oil on both sides. Bake, turning once, until golden on both sides (about 5 minutes).

4 Place the toasted bread in a soup tureen and pour in the hot soup. If adding eggs, use a heatproof tureen, slide eggs into the soup, and bake at 230°C until set (about 3–4 minutes).

7 cups chicken broth

2 beef bones

1 head garlic, separated into cloves, unpeeled, plus 8 cloves, peeled and chopped

4 parsley sprigs

salt and freshly ground pepper

2 1/2–3 tbsp olive oil

1/4 pound cured ham, such as prosciutto, sliced 1/2 cm thick and diced

1 tbsp paprika

1/2 tsp ground cumin

8 bread slices, 5mm thick, from a French baguette

4 large eggs (optional)

serve 4

Thai-Spiked Pumpkin Soup

2 tbsp olive oil
1 large brown onion, chopped
4 cloves garlic, chopped
1 small red birdseye chilli, finely chopped
1/2 bunch coriander
1/2 tsp chilli paste
1 tsp ground cumin
1 tsp turmeric
500g Queensland blue pumpkin, diced
500g butternut pumpkin, diced
500g pumpkin, diced
6 cups chicken stock
400g can coconut milk

serves 8

1 Heat the olive oil in a large saucepan and add the onion and garlic and cook for 10 minutes to caramelise gently. Add the chilli and coriander stems (finely chopped) and stir until fragrant.

2 Add the remaining spices and heat until toasted. Add all the pumpkin pieces and stir to coat with spice mixture. Cover with a lid and cook over a low heat for 30 minutes until the pumpkin is beginning to soften and turn brown. Add just enough stock to cover and stir well.

3 Simmer for 1 hour, then add the coconut milk and simmer for a further 15 minutes. Purée then serve, garnished with extra chillies and coriander.

Russian Cabbage Soup

2 tbsp olive oil

3 large onions, chopped

2 small turnips, peeled and diced

2 white potatoes, peeled and diced

1 small red cabbage, finely sliced

1/2 white cabbage, finely sliced

2 litres chicken or vegetable stock

4 fresh bay leaves (or dry bay leaves if necessary)

2 apples, peeled and finely chopped

3 tbsp fresh dill

4 tbsp sour cream

salt and black pepper to taste

serves 6

1 Heat the oil and sauté the onion until golden, about 5 minutes. Add the diced turnips and potatoes and cook for a further 5 minutes.

2 Add the sliced red and white cabbage, stock, bay leaves and bring to the boil. Simmer for 30 minutes then add the chopped apples and simmer for a further two minutes.

Traditional French Onion Soup

8 large onions
100g butter (or oil)
2 cloves garlic, minced
1 1/2 tbsp flour
1 tbsp sugar
1 litre good quality beef stock
2–3 cups water
1/2 cup red wine
4 tbsp sherry or port
salt and pepper to taste
8 rounds of bread
1/2 cup grated Gruyère
1/2 cup grated Parmesan
1/2 cup finely chopped parsley

serves 8

1 Peel and slice the onions into rounds. Heat the butter (or oil) and sauté the garlic and onions until they are shiny and golden brown, about 15 minutes. Add the flour and stir to allow the flour to absorb the butter residue.

2 Add the sugar, beef stock, water and wine and bring to the boil then simmer for 45 minutes. Add the sherry and simmer 5 minutes more. Add salt and pepper to taste.

3 Grill the bread until golden. Meanwhile, mix the two cheeses and parsley in a bowl. Place a large tablespoon of cheese mixture on each round of grilled bread and grill until cheese is hot and bubbling.

4 Place one round of bread in each soup bowl and then ladle boiling soup over. The crouton will rise to the top of the bowl, serve immediately.

Mexican Chicken Soup

10 cups chicken stock

2 sprigs thyme

1 head (bulb) of garlic, unpeeled

2 fresh (or bottled) jalapeño chillies

3 large tomatoes, diced

2 medium onions

500g cooked chicken meat

1/2 cup chopped coriander

1/2 cup chopped parsley

2 ripe avocados

100g sour cream

juice of 1 lime

serves 10

1 Heat the broth to a simmer with the thyme sprigs and head of garlic, sliced in half horizontally (but not peeled). Simmer for 1 hour. Meanwhile, cut the jalapeño chillies in half and discard the seeds. Mince the chilli and set aside. Dice the tomatoes and onions. Shred the cooked chicken meat.

2 After the soup has simmered for an hour, remove the garlic and thyme sprigs and add the chilli, tomatoes and onions and simmer for a further 10 minutes. Add the shredded chicken meat and simmer for a further minute, then add salt and pepper to taste.

3 To serve, stir through the coriander and parsley then top the soup with finely diced avocado, a dollop of sour cream and a few drops of lime juice.

Beef Udon Noodle Soup (Niku Udon)

85g udon noodles

1 cup udonji, heated

55g eye fillet, sliced very thinly

1 tbsp sliced spring onion greens

1 tbsp cooked tempura batter pieces

1/2 tsp chopped white sesame seeds

serves 1

1 Cook udon noodles in boiling water for 8 minutes, until tender.

2 Pour hot udonji into a serving bowl. Spoon in hot cooked udon noodles.

3 Overlap slices of beef onto the noodles, covering half the bowl. Add spring onions and tempura batter pieces to the soup.

4 Sprinkle sesame seeds over the soup and serve.

Japanese Noodle Soup with Fresh Tuna

570mL fish stock

4 tbsp dark soy sauce

4 tbsp sake or dry sherry

2 tbsp rice or wine vinegar

1 tbsp caster sugar

2 tbsp sesame oil

225g fresh udon noodles

4 tuna steaks, about 145g each, skinned

2 tbsp sesame seeds

fresh coriander to garnish

serves 4

1 Place the stock, soy sauce, sake or sherry, vinegar, sugar and 1 tablespoon of the oil into a saucepan. Bring to the boil and cook, uncovered for 15 minutes, or until reduced by about a third.

2 Meanwhile, prepare the noodles, according to the packet instructions, until tender but still firm to the bite. Brush the tuna steaks with the remaining oil and coat the edges with sesame seeds. Heat a ridged cast-iron grill pan or heavy-based frying pan until very hot. Add the tuna steaks and cook for 2 minutes on each side or until seared.

3 Transfer the noodles to serving bowls, pour over the stock, top with the tuna steaks and garnish with coriander, then serve immediately.

These tuna steaks are seared on the outside but still succulent in the middle. You may cook them a little longer if you like, but take care not to make them too dry.

Spring Onion, Sesame and Shiitake Soup

4 cups chicken stock
2 cups beef stock
55g dried shiitake mushrooms
30g piece fresh ginger, sliced
1 tsp toasted sesame oil
1 tsp five spice powder
1 tbsp teriyaki sauce
2 tbsp mirin
115g button mushrooms, finely sliced
6 spring onions, sliced diagonally
1 tbsp sesame seeds

1 Heat chicken and beef stocks in a saucepan and add shiitake mushrooms and sliced ginger. Bring to the boil then simmer for 5 minutes. Remove from the heat and allow to rest for 40 minutes.

2 Remove mushrooms from the liquid and carefully slice them, discarding stems. Remove ginger from stock and set aside. Line a sieve with some paper towel then pour the stock into the sieve. Allow stock to drain through the sieve, straining out all the grit and sand from the mushrooms. Discard the paper.

3 Return strained stock, ginger and shittake mushrooms to saucepan and bring to a simmer. Add sesame oil, five spice powder, teriyaki sauce, mirin and finely sliced mushrooms and simmer for 10 minutes.

4 Remove ginger then add sliced spring onions.

5 Serve the soup in Japanese bowls, garnished with sesame seeds.

Crispy Buckwheet Noodle Soup with Duck Breast (Age Soba And Kamo Suimono)

125g soba noodles

125g duck breast, cut into 16 thin slices

arrowroot

8 spring onions, white stem only

4 cups udonji

4 sprigs mitsuba

serves 4

1 Cook soba noodles in boiling water for 5–6 minutes, until tender. Drain well.

2 Divide noodles into 4 and shape each into a small ball. Deep fry each ball carefully until golden brown. Take care while frying to retain the shape of each ball. Drain on kitchen paper.

3 Toss each slice of duck breast lightly in arrowroot. Bring a pan of water to the boil and cook the slices for 1–2 minutes.

4 Place spring onions on a hot grill and cook for 1 minute on each side.

5 Heat udonji until boiling. Pour 1 cup into each serving bowl. Top with sliced duck, spring onions, mitsuba sprigs and soba balls.

Index